Beautiful Mandalas
Coloring Book

This book belongs to

_____

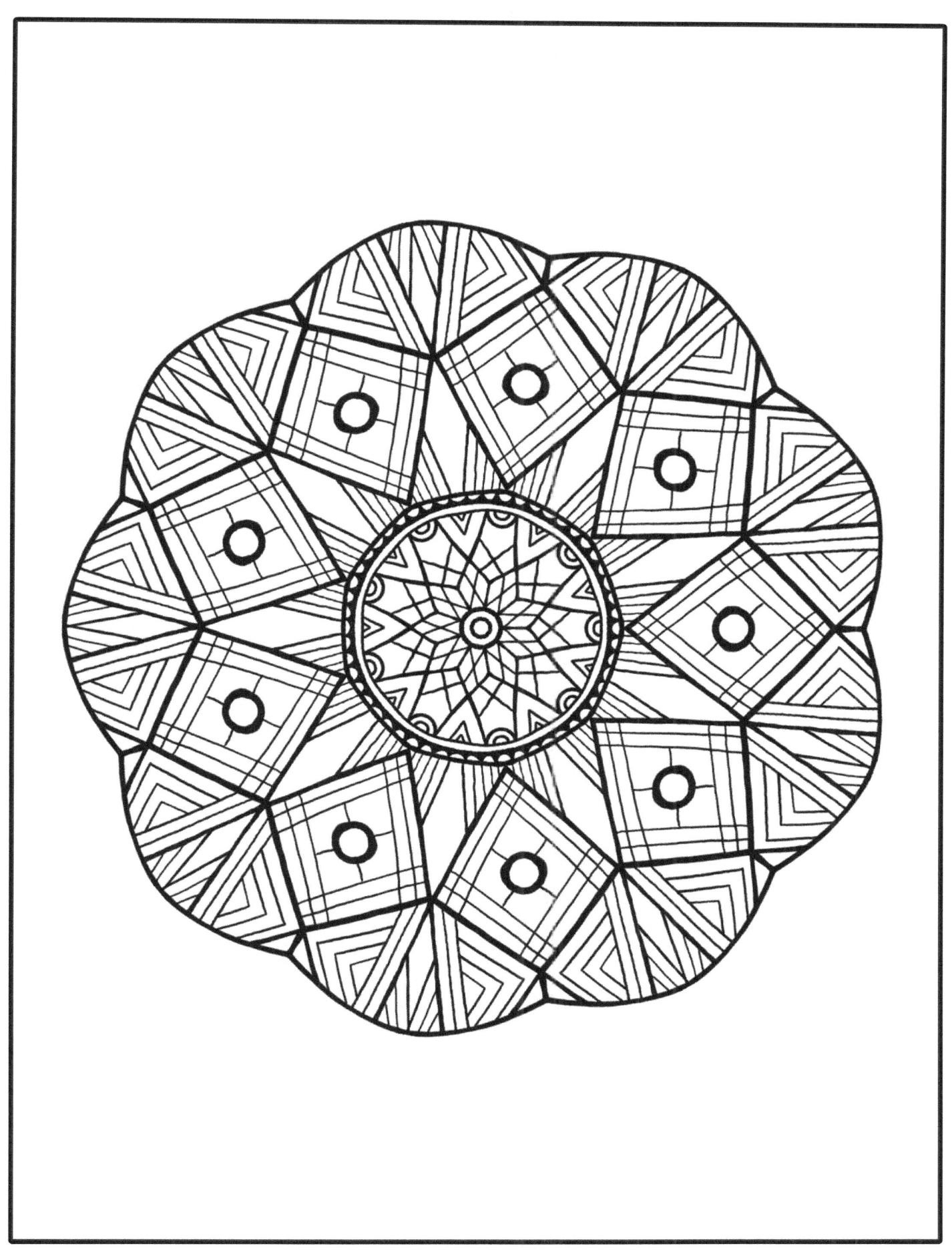

COLOR TEST PAGE

COLOR TEST PAGE

www.ingramcontent.com/pod-product-compliance
Lightning Source LLC
Chambersburg PA
CBHW080453220526
45465CB00006B/2257